BOOK OWNER DET

Thank you so much for your purchase, If you like this book I would greatly appreciate a review. (this will really help me with future sales).

If you are interested in receiving free printable versions of my books and many others, simply scan the QR code below with your phones camera.

This will bring you to my facebook page, where you can receive your free download.

Printed in Great Britain
by Amazon